THE ROOF IS CAVING IN

Matilda Gibbs

with Belle Hansen and Jack Burmeister

CURRENCY PRESS
The performing arts publisher

CURRENT THEATRE SERIES

First published in 2024
by Currency Press Pty Ltd,
Gadigal Land, Suite 310, 46–56 Kippax Street, Surry Hills, NSW 2010, Australia
enquiries@currency.com.au
www.currency.com.au

in association with La Mama Theatre

Typeset by Brighton Gray for Currency Press.
Printed by CanPrint, Canberra, ACT.
Cover features Hayley Edwards and Anna Louey.
Cover image by Darren Gill.
Cover design by Mathias Johanssen.

Currency Press acknowledges the Traditional Owners of the Country on which we live and work. We pay our respects to all Aboriginal and Torres Strait Islander Elders, past and present.

A catalogue record for this book is available from the National Library of Australia

Contents

The Roof is Caving In was first produced by La Mama at La Mama Courthouse Theatre, on the traditional Land of the people of the Kulin Nation, Melbourne, on 8 May 2024, with the following cast and creatives:

HESTER	Marlena Thomson
BRONWYN	Bek Schilling
REAL ESTATE AGENT/VIOLINIST	Joanna Halliday
LOVE INTEREST/ELECTRIC GUITARIST	Linus Finn Mackie
NEIGHBOUR/PIANIST	Karen Yee
HANDYMAN/TROMBONIST	Joshua Mackie
THERAPIST/CLARINETTIST	Daniel Kim

Director, Belle Hansen
Composer and Sound Designer, Jack Burmeister
Lighting Designer, Aron Murray
Stage Manager and Co-Set Designer, Brigette Jennings
Assistant Stage Manager, Jade Hibbert

CHARACTERS

HESTER
BRONWYN
REAL-ESTATE AGENT/VIOLINIST
HANDYMAN/TROMBONIST
NEIGHBOUR/PIANIST
TRUE-CRIME PODCASTER
LOVE INTEREST/ELECTRIC GUITARIST
THERAPIST/CLARINETTIST

This play text went to press before the end of rehearsals and may differ from the play as performed.

SCENE 1. APARTMENT ONBOARDING

The show opens in darkness. Lights come up, revealing a lifeless space with sheets covering furniture items of different shapes and sizes. One by one, the sheets are pulled back. It's a surreal and whimsically impractical environment, where every object stands out in obnoxious cyan blue. Also a part of the furniture, are five instrumentalists, who breathe as one, and only stir when the house calls upon them.

The REAL-ESTATE AGENT/VIOLINIST *sits gracefully on a washing machine, beside a vase filled with cyan flowers. In a blend of speech and a brief, musical interlude, the* REAL-ESTATE AGENT/VIOLINIST *welcomes* HESTER *and* BRONWYN *to their new home. Both are holding boxes filled with all their belongings,* HESTER*'s being orange and* BRONWYN*'s being purple.*

REAL-ESTATE AGENT/VIOLINIST: Hello, hello. Welcome, welcome. Just on time, very punctual! What a promising sign. Here is … and I hope this isn't too pre-emptive to say … your new home. Say it with me. Come on, into the universe. If you didn't believe it now you will. 'New h—' don't be shy, with me now.

REAL-ESTATE AGENT/VIOLINIST, HESTER *and* BRONWYN: 'New home.'

REAL-ESTATE AGENT/VIOLINIST: 'New home.' Oh! How delightful! 'New home', unless of course you use Blu Tack to hang photos which will peel the paint—it will peel the paint so you'll regret that, or hammer into the walls, or fry food. Steaming is fine, frying is a mighty NO. The risk, the inevitable risk: grease splatters, staining, fire hazards, oil! Ever tried removing oil?! Can't be done. Yeah. That would be a breach of our agreement. Our arrangement. Our contract. Refer to page forty-four, it's there. You cannot drag pots and pans, it'll hurt the stove. Suitcases are to be unpacked in the kitchen only, then bagged and tied off in the hallway. For obvious reasons, I know you understand. It's not that we don't trust you, it's just that … Oh! No to peace lilies. Yes to peace and quiet, the walls are thin. Think of your neighbours. You have seven.

REAL-ESTATE AGENT/VIOLINIST *does air-hostess signalling to indicate the neighbours.*

Keep the couch, chuck the couch. The choice is yours. But, it was left behind for a reason. At your own risk.

We care, we *care so deeply about you, oh, so, so, so deeply.* We understand that searching for the right rental property to call home was time-consuming and stressful but that's all over now. You have really hit the jackpot. This place … has a roof. This place has walls. And yes, a door, what a feature. And yes, we care. About *you* and the sanctity of the forever home you wish to make for yourself … for twelve calendar months … give or take … *home.* [*Smiling from ear to ear*] Well, come on, feel it out!

BRONWYN *and* HESTER *take a step inside and are about to put down their belongings.*

Ah, speechless. In awe, I suppose.

The REAL-ESTATE AGENT/VIOLINIST *gestures to a bottle with a crusty ribbon around it and a card stationed next to it simply labelled 'Welcome!'* BRONWYN *approaches and picks it up, it's mostly empty. They shake it, discontented.*

To warm the place up a bit! An ornament.

The REAL-ESTATE AGENT/VIOLINIST *begins an aggressively sanctimonious score, as a house key floats down from the heavens and hovers expectedly in a halo for someone to grab it.* HESTER *and* BRONWYN *speak to each other awkwardly and extremely fast-paced.*

The REAL-ESTATE AGENT/VIOLINIST*'s score comes to a halt… then…*

HESTER: / Bronwyn!
BRONWYN: / Hi—

They both clamp their mouths shut, and politely invite each other through gesture to speak.

A beat.

HESTER: Hello! Hi, yeah I'm Hester. So … one key.
BRONWYN: Yeah …
HESTER: For a two-bed?
BRONWYN: Looks like … and uh, your name's on the lease?

HESTER: Yes ma'am! … Sorry … and um, and your name's on the lease?

BRONWYN: Last I checked, haha.

HESTER: Did they leave the other key somewhere else? Maybe?

BRONWYN: Well, I can't see another halo.

HESTER: What would you prefer—like—

BRONWYN: Oh you know me. Not too fussed on—

HESTER: I don't have a preference either! … Like … / Yeah, let's settle this inside!

BRONWYN: / Happy to nip it in the bud now!

HESTER *and* BRONWYN: Oh!

Both of them look towards the key, wide-eyed. Neither of them take it.

HESTER: So, is this your first … ?

BRONWYN: … Yeah! And … ?

HESTER: Yeah! Me too!

Beat.

HESTER *holds up her hand, offering a rather impulsive high-five. There's a pause, a beat too long.* HESTER *sweats, as does* BRONWYN*, who eventually offers their hand up.*

… So what do you do for study? Are you studying?

BRONWYN: Um—

HESTER: Yeah, are you in the arts? You look artsy!

BRONWYN: [*momentarily offended*] … Why would you … wait no, that's chic … You think I'm free-spirited?

HESTER: Yeah, that was a compliment, sorry!

… / I'm doing a Med degree.

BRONWYN: Geospatial Science degree. Oh! Sorry for int—

HESTER: Oh great! Oh—don't, no, it happens. I'm sorry. Where are you going with that, do you think?

BRONWYN: Oh! Hahahahah not sure … yet.

HESTER: Sorry ah! The acoustics out here. Missed what you were saying.

A lukewarm confusion crosses BRONWYN*'s face. They are outside ...*

BRONWYN: What do—

HESTER: I'm going to be an anaesthetist!

BRONWYN: Wow! Starstruck at future you! I hear they pay anesthesiologists like so / much eventually—

HESTER: Anaesthetists! Sorry, it's anaesthetists—

BRONWYN: Oh sorry! I thought they were the same thing—

HESTER: They're not. They're different, but all good! What are your contact hours like?

BRONWYN: Intense. But, the pre-recorded lectures are going to be my best friend! Planning on working from home as much as I can.

HESTER: Intense, yeah, intense.

Beat.

Ah, oops sorry! I pre-empted the question. Like, I went too early, that was rude. I should have let you ask the question first.

BRONWYN: Oh yeah! The hours are also big too… for you?

HESTER: Yeah! But that's perfectly A-OKAY with me! I don't think I'll ever miss a day. Being in a hospital is my happy place!

Beat.

I'll be doing my classes in person. Like a good girl!

Beat.

Early starts, ugh!

BRONWYN: Well, I'm a morning person, so I can see you off.

HESTER: How nice! Thank you.

HESTER *and* BRONWYN *both reach for the key, stop short, and* HESTER *holds out her hand again for another high-five. She sighs disappointedly at her own repeated awkward gesture.* BRONWYN *high-fives her again.*

What do you do recreationally?

BRONWYN: Recreationally—

HESTER: Oh god, listen to me! Hes, this isn't a job interview! Hahahahahahhah—

HESTER *and* BRONWYN *look at the key again. Then back at each other.*

BRONWYN: … Uh recreationally. Right—

HESTER: For fun!
BRONWYN: I like walking.
HESTER: Oh cool.
BRONWYN: But not recreationally really—
HESTER: Oh it's not fun?
BRONWYN: Well, no I love it. But it's more like training. I racewalk.
HESTER: Oh that's wow! Like, I've seen videos of people taking part in that, but never in person! It always felt like such a … phenomenon! Like, is it even real?! You're so much cooler than all those basic runners out there!

Beat.

… Yeah I run, I just think it's the easiest way to get up in the morn—

BRONWYN *has instinctually refocused on the key which still floats above them, unclaimed.* HESTER *stops short, following their gaze.*

BRONWYN: It's so nice out here.
HESTER: Yeah—
BRONWYN: I hope it's the same inside.
HESTER: By the seaside!!
BRONWYN: Uh …
HESTER: No, that was—I was—the key to getting up early. It's an alarm sound. It tickles my brain in just the right way, makes me pretty wired. But a serene wired … Um … so shall we … ?

They both pull out their key rings.

HESTER *and* BRONWYN: Oh sorry!
BRONWYN: I like your key ring.
HESTER: Thanks. I thought there was no other word for this tone other than cream, right? But the shock of my life: papaya whip! A pastel orange. Cushy to touch, I like that it's round so I can use it as a stress ball. When situations … stress me out. Squish squish. Yours?
BRONWYN: Purple. It's just … it's purple. Small and compact!

Silence.

BRONWYN *can't take the back-and-forth any longer.*

May I?

HESTER: [*squeezing ball keychain*] Sure!

BRONWYN *grabs the key, relieved.*

SCENE 2. SNOWBALLING SIMULTANEOUS MONOLOGUE

HESTER *and* BRONWYN *enter their new home. They are both immediately stumped at the state of the place.*

BRONWYN: Wow, it's … / so snug and beautiful.

HESTER: Really fucking dirty—

Beat.

HESTER *abruptly grabs the couch and moves it across, slotting it somewhere else, somewhere more to her liking.* BRONWYN *recoils at the pomeranian-sized dead rats that appear as the couch is drawn away. They pick them up and open the window to fling them out, all while* HESTER *isn't looking.*

Oh … um sorry was that—you know what, I shouldn't— [*Beginning to move item back*] I should have asked you …

HESTER *pauses and looks at* BRONWYN*, silently hoping her change to the space can remain.*

BRONWYN: [*smiling sweetly*] No, it's okay.

HESTER *moves the furniture item back pridefully. To* HESTER*, the place just became ten times better. The drag of furniture on the floor prompts the house to respond in a disgruntled, impatient moan. It sounds almost supernatural.*

HESTER: Whoa.

BRONWYN: Oh, she's hungry. Or pissed.

HESTER *continues inspecting the place.*

HESTER: [*gasping*] It's a Wednesday.

BRONWYN: Right!

HESTER: It's a bin day, days for bins.

BRONWYN: Bin day! Sure, I'll do them. First official errand.

HESTER: Thank you.

BRONWYN *exits with the bins.* HESTER *begins to unpack the space. She discovers the trundle beds. Along the inner sides of each one, there is a perfectly jagged slice running from headboard to footboard. She clocks the more desired bedroom, and she cannot help herself. She's unpacking, scattering specks of orange around her claimed space.*

HESTER *notices, again, the jagged bed side. Realisation dawns and she drags one bed across and slots it into the other like a puzzle, making one double bed. They've been had.* BRONWYN *can be heard re-entering, causing* HESTER *to separate the beds and reposition them.* BRONWYN *tries to conceal their shock at the sudden presence of orange.*

Now this is snug and beautiful!

BRONWYN: Ha! Yeah, such a great space hey.

The more desired bedroom: it catches both HESTER *and* BRONWYN*'s eye. It, too, is very orange. They advance for it, then halt. Both choose to ignore what has happened in* BRONWYN*'s absence.*

HESTER: Have you checked out the other bedroom?

BRONWYN: Yeah! You?

HESTER: Yeah! You? Oh sorry, you—yes you have.

BRONWYN: … / Earlier you said—

HESTER: … / The dimensions over there are just perf—

Beat.

BRONWYN: Earlier you said you'll be going onto campus a lot—

HESTER: Yeah I will! Hoping to create the very BEST working environment for myself, when I am / home—

BRONWYN: Home not that often though, right?

Beat.

Intense hours, the words you used? In-person attendance isn't as mandatory for me. But god, the study hours'll be rough. Guess I'll have to make sure I've got a cushy study space—

HESTER: How's the key going on your amethyst keychain?

BRONWYN: Purple, just purple—

HESTER: … Yeah … my papaya whip's light. And lonely.

BRONWYN: [*folding*] … That room over there, it's just perfect for me. Is it—may I take … that one?

HESTER: Oh my god, sure, it doesn't matter to me either way!

> BRONWYN *reluctantly leaves the preferred bedroom and settles for the tight cranny at the other end of the apartment. They unpack their belongings, sprinkling the area with purple items. They both sit in their respective spaces, which appear to be too small for them.*

BRONWYN: [*dramatically slumping*] Well, I'm officially settled!

HESTER: Oh, GREAT! Wow, I feel fantastic now. Just the thought of getting this place scrubbed up is giving me goosebumps.

> HESTER *shows her goosebumps.* BRONWYN *looks around at what they believe is a fairly clean space.*

BRONWYN: Where is / it mess—

HESTER: The best place to start? True, what a dump. Well, there's the grease splatters and the floors and when the light hits that shelf just right you can see the layers and layers of dust. And no doubt, we need to … um … / THROW … away the couch—

BRONWYN: THROW … a party—what?

HESTER: YES, PARTY!

BRONWYN: Oh thank GOD—

HESTER: Reading your mind there—

BRONWYN: There is nothing—

HESTER: Nothing—

BRONWYN: Nothing I love more than PARTIES—

HESTER: And we need to get warm—

BRONWYN: The warmest—

HESTER: With all our friends—

BRONWYN: Our own liquor with our own money—

HESTER: BYE Mum and Dad—

BRONWYN: Love a little fat lamb—

HESTER: I don't drink—

BRONWYN: You must be very dehydrated—

HESTER: But I am heavily caffeinated—

BRONWYN: Give me three shots of the good stuff—

HESTER: I love being an extrovert—

BRONWYN: then BAM! ENFP, that's me!

HESTER: I love people, dancing, loud noises, destroyed furniture, overshares, courting—

BRONWYN: Guest list, / HUGE—

HESTER: MASSIVE—

BRONWYN: / MASSIVE—

HESTER: / HUGE—

HESTER *and* BRONWYN: [*simultaneously*] Because of all the friends I have!

The musicians play from their statued positions, a musical styling: pizzicato and percussion. What proceeds is a monologue delivered with identical emotional, rhythmic and physical delivery. Together, they share their internal monologue.

[*Simultaneously*] Massive? Huge?! What friends am I referring to?

BRONWYN: / Oh! Actually I have a few …

HESTER: / I only know, like three people, and my parents think I'm a loose end with the personality of expired milk.

BRONWYN: But they're all taking a gap year and travelling the world … gross.

HESTER *and* BRONWYN: [*simultaneously*] What am I doing right now? I'm not built for hosting. I haven't got the—

HESTER: / —sociability for this kind of thing!

BRONWYN: / —organisation for this kind of thing!

HESTER *and* BRONWYN: [*simultaneously*] It's an innate quality that I simply don't have.

HESTER: It's just not in my make-up, OKAY?

BRONWYN: Red flag, red flag—

HESTER *and* BRONWYN: [*simultaneously*] Abort, abort! Why did I just do that? I don't want this, I really don't want this!

HESTER: I mean, like where, where, where …

HESTER *and* BRONWYN: [*simultaneously*] Where do I start? Sharing the event, what do you name it?

BRONWYN: 'Brrrrr it's pretty chilly up in here, come help us warm up?'

HESTER: 'Meet our new homie!'

BRONWYN: Pretty sure that's too many letters—

HESTER *and* BRONWYN: [*simultaneously*] And the money, with what funds are we doing this? Are they rich? Hmm … are they rich? No, no, not with that fit—stop— [*Slapping own hand*] Being judgemental is like vaping …

BRONWYN: / It's addictive and feels good but ruins the insides.

HESTER: It's disgusting, disgusting and ruins the insides.

HESTER *and* BRONWYN: Okay worst-case, worst-case, nothing to their name, nothing to give, how are we affording drinks? And how are we affording snacks, even the chips on clearance? Do we go halfsies? [*Slapping own hand*] Halfsies?! What am I? Twelve?

BRONWYN: God, I need my vape.

HESTER *and* BRONWYN: [*simultaneously*] And dietaries, no doubt there'll be dietaries because who nowadays can process dairy or gluten from mouth to colon without it becoming the calendar event of the following evening? Pescatarians … I feel like pescetarianism is spiking in popularity … NO MEATS. But like, little bits of meat here and there because I'm terrified of what meateaters'll do to me if I stripped them of their rights. What else do people eat?

HESTER *and* BRONWYN *in a panic turn to each other wide eyed, oblivious to the other's frantic internal monologue.*

[*Simultaneously*] No don't don't say anyth— well now I'm staring … and yep I should probably speak now and say something so cool—

HESTER: / Mastery is me, I'm a great chef, quaint, cute foods with croquettes and CROQUEMBOUCHE—

BRONWYN: / Dishes are scary, like I love Master CHEF but please don't make me cook, no crumpets or CROQUEMBOUCHE—

Beat.

HESTER *and* BRONWYN: [*simultaneously*] Yes, I'll make the croquembouche!

HESTER *and* BRONWYN *turn back out to the audience.*

[*Simultaneously*] God how pathetic, a croquembouche? I can't even bake and who would eat a tower of dough—

I'm going to mess this up. What to wear? Definitely not anything from the outdated cesspool of eras that is my wardrobe. And the unnecessary money and stress for a new outfit to just end up moth-eaten in a cave in my bedroom somewhere.

Oh, and what about the neighbours? The neighbours, they'll hate us before we give them a proper reason to.

HESTER: No, they can't hate me, I'll see them every Wednesday night when the bins go out—

BRONWYN: They're gonna think our playlist is an absolute crock of sh—

HESTER *and* BRONWYN: [*simultaneously*] NO, I won't be able to stand the tension.

HESTER: How am I going to be able to control the noise, keep the music volume in check? The walls are thin!

Beat.

/ Oh no …

BRONWYN: / Oh no … no Premium. I've got. / No. Premium. The ads. THE ADS.

HESTER: No.

HESTER *and* BRONWYN: [*simultaneously*] They'll get back at us for this. Oh god, they'll get back at us for this, they're gonna stomp their feet and slam on the walls and steal our mail!

This'll be a disaster, I can't do this, I can't do this.

HESTER *and* BRONWYN *have unravelled into tears.*

Beat.

NO. Quit the pity party.

BRONWYN: Get a subscription, you loser.

HESTER: If anyone can keep the noise levels in check, it's you, Hes!

HESTER *and* BRONWYN: You will NOT lose to MUSIC.

They face each other and out comes:

HESTER: I've got a decibel metre!

BRONWYN: I've got Spotify Premium!

HESTER *and* BRONWYN: Now that's a party!

HESTER *pulls out some paper and begins to write, equations and all.*

HESTER: Four to six months.

BRONWYN: Sorry what?

HESTER: I've run the logistics. At least from my end. Everything from budgeting, to having all the facilities in order.

BRONWYN: So … half a year … huh. Before we can have a housewarming?

All they both want to do is stop this snowballing idea, but ...

HESTER: … House luke-warming!

BRONWYN: Even better—

HESTER: It'll be the party of the century—

BRONWYN: No-one will know what hit 'em!

HESTER *reaches for more paper and starts to aggressively write down a list. The lights glaze slightly, as* BRONWYN *prances about the apartment, unpacking all their belongings. They finish with a baby pot plant, which still has a lot of growing to do.*

SCENE 3. HANDYMAN HELP

It is bright.

BRONWYN *sits, with big noise-cancelling headphones on, listening to a university lecture.* HESTER *enters, placing the borrowed key under a mat. She notices the kitchen mess, followed by the relentless blaring of a smoke alarm. The* INSTRUMENTALISTS *all cover their ears and squirm, as one extremely uncomfortable organism.*

BRONWYN: / Hey!

HESTER: / Yeah, fine! Busy—really—I was almost late because of the road works happ— sorry Bronwyn, do you hear that?

BRONWYN: Oh yeah, I knowwww.

HESTER: … The smoke alarm?

BRONWYN: Yeah, it's so obnoxious!

HESTER: Right. What happened, do you know? Is it to do with us / or are—

BRONWYN: It might have been the chorizo—

HESTER: Oh! Did you have the fan on—

BRONWYN: Actually, the sauce was a spattering, burning mess. So that would have done it for sure—

HESTER: The fan, did you have it on?

BRONWYN: Doesn't work.

HESTER: Oh, that's weird. You pressed the right—like—you know that you need to press knobs right?

BRONWYN: Um, yeah! Yeah, I know that.

HESTER: … How long has it been … of just— [*miming the alarm-blaring noise*]

BRONWYN: Oh … um. A while.

HESTER: Okay well … um, would you like me to turn it off? Unless you like, enjoy—you need—you're using … it?

BRONWYN: Oh, yeah no I'm not, it's not pleasant. You can turn that off.

HESTER *drags a chair to the smoke alarm.*

… Thanks … Thanking you.

The blaring abruptly cuts off.

HESTER: What?

BRONWYN: Oh. Th— um, sorry, nothing …

BRONWYN *places their headphones back on.* HESTER *notices the sink is leaking.*

HESTER: Um, heyyyy. Have you noticed the sink is leaking?

BRONWYN *does their best to interpret what* HESTER *is saying with their headphones cutting off sound.*

HESTER: The SINK.

HESTER *approaches the sink and aggressively points.* BRONWYN *removes their headphones.*

The sink is leaking! Did you notice?

BRONWYN*'s face changes, they are anxious. They did notice.*

[*Lobotomy smiling*] I can phone … for a repair?

BRONWYN: Can I help in any way?

HESTER: No, it's okay!

HESTER *dials for the* REAL-ESTATE AGENT/VIOLINIST, *whose phone rings, as sounded by the* NEIGHBOUR/PIANIST. *The* REAL-ESTATE AGENT/VIOLINIST *looks at their phone and lets it ring ... and ring ... and ring.*

No luck.

Pause.

BRONWYN *places their headphones back on, resigned.* HESTER *notices a mislabeled plant.*

[*Whispering*] That's not even a Devil's Ivy, it's a philodendron.

HESTER *dials again.* BRONWYN *removes their headphones, obliging. No-one answers.*

Pause.

BRONWYN *places their headphones on.* HESTER *dials again.* BRONWYN *removes their headphones ... again. No answer.*

Beat.

I'll call later.

Pause.

BRONWYN *finally thinks it is safe to place back on their headphones.*

However, HESTER *pulls out a laptop and begins typing an email. Her face is illuminated by the screen light, much like* BRONWYN*'s with their laptop.*

[*Muttering*] Okay, okay, okay … 'Dear … Mrs'—Wait—'Miss … Ma'am … Madam … Mrs … Mx'—Goddammit—

BRONWYN *watches as* HESTER *flounders through the start of her email. It's an uncomfortable thing to witness, and they feel obligated to help.*

BRONWYN: Is she married?

HESTER*'s head snaps up.*

HESTER: Pardon?
BRONWYN: Marital status?
HESTER: … Unknown—uh—I'm not sure.
BRONWYN: Okay, well then.
HESTER: Oh.
BRONWYN: Yeah. / 'Dear Miss'—
HESTER: 'Dear Ms' … Sorry? Did you say Miss? Or Ms?
BRONWYN: [*self-correcting*] Relationship status, unknown. So, 'Ms'—
HESTER: ZZZ. Ms?

BRONWYN: ZZZ.
HESTER: [*taking a breath*] 'Dear … Ms', new line, 'I am—'

BRONWYN *shuts their own laptop.*

BRONWYN: 'Dear', too formal?
HESTER: Ah, yeah. Personable. 'Hey', 'Hi', 'Heya Ms—
BRONWYN: Too juvenile?
HESTER: 'Greetings'—
BRONWYN: And salutations—
HESTER: 'Howdy there'—
BRONWYN: Right up my alley but probably not up theirs—

HESTER *starts to type again, singing the first line of the chorus of Taylor Swift's* Anti-hero.

HESTER: 'Just kidding, it's our sink.'
BRONWYN: Yes, great, good I like that.

HESTER *sings the first line of the chorus of Taylor Swift's* Anti-hero *again.*

HESTER: 'Just kidding, it's our / sink.'
BRONWYN: 'Tap'—

Beat.

HESTER: Well, it's a / synonym.
BRONWYN: Synonym, yeah.
HESTER: Right—
BRONWYN: In case you needed more options. The power of choice.
HESTER: Right.
BRONWYN: 'Faucet'—
HESTER: Wow, right okay, three choices.
BRONWYN: You're welcome—
HESTER: Yeah, I don't feel all that powerful Bronwyn! :)
BRONWYN: Oh / sorry—
HESTER: Sorry—no … thank you!

Beat.

HESTER *sings the first line of the chorus of Taylor Swift's* Anti-hero *again.*

HESTER: 'Just kidding, it's our sink.'

We, Hester and Bronwyn, tenant and … tenant'—

BRONWYN: 'Bronwyn and Hester'… Alphabetical?

HESTER: 'have recently moved into this fine abode'—

BRONWYN: I also question the wording of 'fine abode', like—oh—sorry to interrupt, but can I / recommend that we—

HESTER: Hold on, sorry I've got a fix.

BRONWYN: Oh—

HESTER continues to frantically type, trying to catch up. BRONWYN points to a place in the email.

Maybe make light of how much we've loved living here so far—

HESTER: 'We'd like to begin by saying that we have enjoyed our stay so far'—

'that we've really taken to this establishment'—

BRONWYN: 'these facilities'—

HESTER: 'this living arrangement'—

BRONWYN: 'our new home'—

HESTER: 'and we'd like to extend our / thank—

BRONWYN: 'gratitude'—

HESTER: ' … itude—that of all the applications submitted for this property'—

BRONWYN: 'of all the wannabe tenants'—

HESTER: 'you picked us'—

BRONWYN: 'you chose us' / reword—

HESTER: reword—

HESTER *and* BRONWYN: 'you selected us'—

BRONWYN: 'you pleasured us'—

HESTER: 'However'—

BRONWYN: Yes, 'despite this'—

HESTER: 'I have noticed'—

BRONWYN: 'It's caught our attention'—

HESTER: 'that the sink is leaking'—

BRONWYN: 'in need of immediate assistance'—

HESTER: 'I'd argue it's gushing'—

BRONWYN: 'there's a fungus among us'—

HESTER: 'like, notify the Bureau of Meteorology Weather'—

BRONWYN: 'and that fungus is a broken faucet'—

HESTER: 'because there's a storm comin''—
BRONWYN: 'torrential'—
HESTER: 'We aren't familiar with the required course of action'—
BRONWYN: 'but we understand that you can authorise and arrange a repair'—
HESTER: 'as soon as is possible'—
BRONWYN: 'for the sake of our poor / faucet'—
HESTER: 'sink'—
BRONWYN: 'Thank you for for sparing the time to read this'—
HESTER: 'We have the privilege of having a flexible schedule'—
BRONWYN: 'and you probably don't'—
HESTER: 'well … till next time'—
BRONWYN: 'we'll be at your beck and call'—
HESTER: 'Hester'—
BRONWYN: 'Bronwyn'—

HESTER *signs off, sends the email and shuts her laptop.*

The doorbell abruptly rings. HESTER *stays glued to the couch, as* BRONWYN *answers the door.*

The HANDYMAN/TROMBONIST *enters the space.*

Hello!

HANDYMAN/TROMBONIST: You reached out … about a sink?
BRONWYN: [*smiling sweetly*] … I'm sorry—

HANDYMAN/TROMBONIST *points to the sink, an asking remark.*

Oh, how did … Who did you—um. Right, well don't let me stop you.

BRONWYN *follows the handyman to the sink and fidgets as he gets to work.* HESTER *starts to get up then suddenly thinks better of it and sits. She doesn't know where to look.*

HESTER: Need a water?

HANDYMAN/TROMBONIST *shakes head.*

Silence ensues.

Uh, okay, okay—uh Bronwyn? Would you like a drink?
BRONWYN: Yeah sure … uh thanks.

HESTER *rises, grabs a glass and realises, the sink is of course, undergoing repair. She stands dumbfounded, crammed in the kitchen area with the* HANDYMAN/TROMBONIST *and* BRONWYN.

Silence once again. Something catches HESTER*'s eye.*

HESTER: … How was your pasta?

BRONWYN: Oh, whoa, you know I had pasta?

HESTER: That's it on the counter right? [*Gesturing to the mess in the kitchen*]

BRONWYN: Oh, I'll get to that.

HESTER:[*masking disgust*] Vintage—

HANDYMAN/TROMBONIST: Won't be long.

The HANDYMAN/TROMBONIST, *crouched facing the sink, begins a musical interlude, indicating they're hard at work making repairs.*

HESTER *still eyes the pasta. It's the last push she needs to reveal a list that she wrote weeks ago.*

HESTER: Hey … so. I was thinking, force of habit I guess, but there are a few things … I do. How would you feel about house rules?

BRONWYN: Oh … absolutely!

Both BRONWYN *and* HESTER *are extremely aware of the stranger in their private space.* HESTER *attaches the rules to the fridge with magnets.*

[*Reading*] 'Clean up after yourself immediately', classic. 'Lock up at night', yep, makes sense, safety always. 'Check the shower heads daily. The cameras are getting smaller and smaller.' Oh. 'Chores involving house upkeep to be on a rotating roster'—

HESTER: Including bins!

BRONWYN: Absolutely. 'Don't leave laundry in the washing machine.'

HESTER: It'll rot.

Beat.

Apparently!

BRONWYN: 'Diamond, not squares'. Sorry?

HESTER: The cushions! A decorative thing.

BRONWYN: Oh, okay I follow. [*Reading*] 'No couch indents, unless you're on day two of your period'—

HESTER: That day is hell!
BRONWYN: [*forcing a smile*] No notes!
And there's room down here for me to add some?

Beat.

HESTER: … Fire away!

BRONWYN *goes to write, hesitates, then scribbles something down.*

Then, the HANDYMAN/TROMBONIST *coughs.*

BRONWYN: [*refocusing*] Want to go to a party?

HESTER*'s eyes widen in awkward panic.*

[*Shrugging*] COME. Our party. It's a housewarming, if you're one for the details.

HESTER: Sorry! That … that—I know that sounds weird coming from two people you've just met! But you are … welcome back—uh to come!

Pause.

We won't be paying you this time though!

HESTER *laughs at her joke attempt.* BRONWYN *joins in and the two obnoxiously laugh away the silence.*

Sorry, this must be quite the offer to get from a client. While your head's buried in a clogged sink. Like, you're extracting mouldy food from a tailpiece / and you're—

BRONWYN: [*quietly confused*] Tailpiece / what's a tailpiece—
HESTER: —tightening that ol' slip nut, and we love your presence *SO MUCH* that we just have to have you back!

Pause.

For street cred!

The music ceases and the HANDYMAN/TROMBONIST *rises, finished with his work.*

HANDYMAN/TROMBONIST: M'kay.
HESTER: [*awkwardly*] Yay!
BRONWYN: See you there!

The HANDYMAN/TROMBONIST *packs up and farewells both* HESTER *and* BRONWYN, *returning to the shower and resetting their position.* HESTER *and* BRONWYN *follow them and share a collective sigh of relief when the* HANDYMAN/TROMBONIST *officially leaves the space.*

Beat.

HESTER *offers a high five.*

HESTER: … Proud of us.

BRONWYN *returns the high-five.*

The rules will just be on the fridge if you forget any of them! Especially rule number three … rotating roster for chores!

BRONWYN: Okay great, thanks.

BRONWYN *returns to the couch, placing headphones back on.*

HESTER: [*whispering and hyping herself up*] Bins, bins, bins. I did it last week and the week before. It's bin night please please can you please take out the— [*Practically screaming*] IT'S WEDNESDAY.

BRONWYN *is startled and removes their headphones.*

BRONWYN: WOOO WEDNESDAY! Happy hump!

BRONWYN *puts back on their headphones.* HESTER *takes out the bins herself.*

NEIGHBOUR/PIANIST: Afternoon!

HESTER: Afternoon!

NEIGHBOUR/PIANIST: Ah yes, Wednesday!

HESTER: Yeah!

NEIGHBOUR/PIANIST: Thank you, I always need the reminder!

The lights snap off, inviting only a natural moonlight into the space. Time jumps.

SCENE 4. SLEEP TIGHT

Both HESTER *and* BRONWYN *are asleep. There's only the sound of* HESTER*'s podcast, muffled in her headphones.*

TRUE-CRIME PODCASTER: So that night she got ready for bed, like normal, they said goodnight to her like normal, and she went to sleep.

A silhouette of the LOVE INTEREST/ELECTRIC GUITARIST *rises behind the window. They begin hammering on it.*

But then, in the middle of the night, they heard a really loud banging noise. It sounded as if someone else was in the house and had slammed a glass door really really hard.

HESTER *wakes up, and is immediately on high alert.*

And you can all probably understand how startling it is to hear a sudden noise from inside your house in the middle of the night. It's incredibly disorienting. It leaves you wondering if you ever heard anything at all. If it was real. Then you hear another sound and now you're really awake and you weren't imagining anything. Someone's inside and suddenly you know every entry and exit point. You're tethered to your bed, and you're watching the door. You wait. You want to do the noble thing and grab something. Or hide. But all you can do is wait. The banging continues. And it's coming from their room. And then it stops. There's a silence. Not the settled kind. So she got up to check on them.

HESTER *stands, rubbing her tired eyes, and investigates the sound.*

She lifts the covers, twisting out of bed. Her feet meet with the ground and—

BRONWYN *appears and opens up the window, letting in the* LOVE INTEREST/ELECTRIC GUITARIST. *They lock eyes.*

BRONWYN: What are you doing here?

HESTER *freezes, listening in. The true-crime podcast continues.* BRONWYN *takes out a camera and moves away to take a photo of the* LOVE INTEREST/ELECTRIC GUITARIST. *He starts to move toward them.*

[*Urgently*] Don't come any closer.

TRUE-CRIME PODCASTER: Someone has infiltrated your home, and they are hurting your friend—

HESTER: [*to self*] They're not really my friend, do I do something?

TRUE-CRIME PODCASTER: … They are hurting your associate, and you know you have to act.

BRONWYN *snaps a photo, approaches and gestures to the guitar, begging him to play for them.*

BRONWYN: I'll do anything. Just please!

The LOVE INTEREST/ELECTRIC GUITARIST, *teasing, saunters away from them.*

HESTER, *panicked, frantically searches for something to use as a weapon.*

TRUE-CRIME PODCASTER: Anything sharp, you think. Where can I find anything sharp? To jab at their hands, pierce their eyeballs, stab them in the stomach, skewer them from arse to skull—

HESTER: [*relishing the thought*] Like a human kebab.

TRUE-CRIME PODCASTER: But you're wasting time looking for that perfect pointy weapon. No. Something heavy and blunt, for a mighty defensive set of blows.

HESTER*'s eyes settle on a lamp.*

So it's late at night and you're dressed for bed but there's a danger close by and you're probably going to die. Think to yourself … Do you really want to die wearing kitty pyjama pants, with a bedhead and chapped lips?

HESTER *stops in her tracks, gripping a lamp like it's a baseball bat. A moment of pause. Then she springs into action, changing outfits, neatening up her hair and even adding lipgloss. All this because, if she's going to die, she wants to look drop-dead gorgeous.*

Weapon at the ready, you creep toward the danger … but surely not before considering the obvious. What's your swing look like when the threat is inches from you, finally staring you down?

HESTER *practises different versions of an attack with her weapon of choice. An uppercut. Right hook. Left hook. Cord swings. Cord whips.*

Now you're ready, finally ready for whoever decided to interrupt your REM sleep by breaking into the lion's den.

HESTER *creeps forward. She's never been more ready in her life.*

BRONWYN: You like it? I love it.

The LOVE INTEREST/ELECTRIC GUITARIST *turns to* BRONWYN. *Yeah, now he wants to play.*

TRUE-CRIME PODCASTER: And finally, vantage point for your attack. Find. Your. Vantage point.

HESTER *leaps into the space hopping from counter to furniture, revealing herself.*

HESTER: VILLAIN!

BRONWYN *jumps back, scared out of their mind, and the* LOVE INTEREST/ELECTRIC GUITARIST *pulls them behind him, a protector.* HESTER *stops in her tracks, crouched with a lamp looking dishevelled.*

BRONWYN: … Evening.

Beat.

HESTER: … I'm just grabbing some midnight delight! Milk.

HESTER *jumps down and fumbles with the lamp before cradling it and letting the cord drag along the floor. She grabs herself a glass of milk from the fridge.*

[*Avoiding eye contact*] As you were.

HESTER *scurries off to bed.*

BRONWYN: That was my housemate … She's … Exams are coming up, so … And you know you don't have to come in through the window any more, right? This is my own place. I've got my own place now!

TRUE-CRIME PODCASTER: Don't forget. 'Kiss with no regret. Neutralise that threat.' I'll be back after a quick sponsor.

The LOVE INTEREST/ELECTRIC GUITARIST *launches into some riffs, spontaneity in his playing.* BRONWYN *ushers him more into the space which lights up, blinding* HESTER, *who has tucked herself back up in bed.*

SCENE 5. I'LL RACE YA

It's bright, afternoon bright.

HESTER *emerges into a rumpled space with her laptop, wearing work headphones. Her top half is glammed in a full fairy-princess look, whilst on her bottom half, she wears tracksuit pants. She sighs as she inspects the mess, itching to clean. As she gets to work,* BRONWYN *enters, the* LOVE INTEREST/ELECTRIC GUITARIST *at their side.*

BRONWYN: Morning!
HESTER: Hi!!! :)
BRONWYN: Coffee for him again. Hope that's okay?
HESTER: It's always a yes, Bronwyn.

Beat.

BRONWYN: Did we wake you last night?
HESTER: A little bit.
BRONWYN: Big day today?
HESTER: [*cynically laughing*] Yeah, shame about our lack of zees.

BRONWYN *tries to repair the tension, as they make a shitty instant coffee.*

BRONWYN: Working another birthday party?
HESTER: No. A kid's cat ran out onto the road and got mowed down. The parents think this'll help him forget.
BRONWYN: Oh no.

Beat.

HESTER *places back on her headphones.*

You know how much I froth a bit of caffeine.
HESTER: Kathleen?
BRONWYN: No, caffeine.
HESTER: Yeah, I'm ready when you are!
BRONWYN: Oh.
HESTER: I'll be talking about my weekend with Princess Glinda and the glitter goblins.

Beat.

Who's alive?

Beat.

Oh—Wasn't it a clean … swipe?

Beat.

Wow. Well, eight lives now.

BRONWYN: Okay, I'm off.

HESTER: Cancelled, okay! Glad to know he's feeling better!

BRONWYN *delivers a coffee to* LOVE INTEREST/ELECTRIC GUITARIST, *who slips them a gift: guitar pic. They appreciate the gesture, but hand it back.*

BRONWYN: Aw. Thank you. Really. My hands will get clammy, so keep it warm for me. And stay as long as you want, okay? Bye.

BRONWYN *leaves for their racewalk training.*

HESTER: Yes, I can still do his birthday and his kindergarten graduation too.

Beat.

See you then, okay. Hahahahaha yay! Bye!

HESTER *removes her headphones.*

Where's Bronwyn?

LOVE INTEREST/ELECTRIC GUITARIST *shrugs. He goes back to playing and sipping on coffee.*

Beat.

… Okay.

She can't stay here.

Okay. Bye. Hope there's room on the roads for two athletes!

HESTER *finds something to duck behind for some privacy and removes her princess costume, ready for her run. On her way out,* HESTER *stops, turns.*

Can you reset the couch when you're done? Like, bring back the fluffiness and the … the bounce, you know, like get rid of the buttocks indent. And that pillow just goes back over it. Diamond, not square! And you can take the mug, like you can just keep that. We won't need that, um, anymore … yeah, just refer to the fridge if you're lost. Thank you, please— [*Malfunctioning*] Please, thank you.

The LOVE INTEREST/ELECTRIC GUITARIST *is left alone on stage. He pulls out a cigarette and purple smoke wafts from it. He finishes his coffee. He resets the couch, as instructed. He handwashes the mug and puts it back. He notices the washing machine has finished its cycle, so he hangs up* BRONWYN*'s clothes for them. He collects their dirty laundry, taking the time to smell a sock of theirs. He catches their scent and rubs the garment all over his face, breathing them in. Then, he eats it. He recollects the dirty laundry and begins a new machine cycle.*

The live INSTRUMENTALISTS *start to rouse in response to the sound of the washing machine. The beat of the chugging acts as an impetus for them all to play, its composition insinuating a passage of time. The lights dim and fade back up, catching* HESTER *staring at the door as she removes her running shoes. The light dims again and on its fade up,* HESTER *is there yet again trying to put on her running shoes. She stands, as if waiting for someone, morningstar in hand.* BRONWYN *emerges, prepped for their racewalk.*

BRONWYN: Whoa, hey.
HESTER: You're heading off then?
BRONWYN: … Yeah. You?
HESTER: Yeah. You've got the key to get back in, so.

BRONWYN *takes out their headphones and places them arounf their neck.*

Beat.

It doesn't worry you that you can't hear your surroundings?
BRONWYN: No, not particularly.
HESTER: …
BRONWYN: Are you?
HESTER: … No. Not worried, no.

Lights out.

SCENE 6. I DREAMED A DREAM

The lights settle again and a house plant has become noticeably larger in size.

BRONWYN *is seated with laptop lights blaring on their face.*

THERAPIST/CLARINETTIST: What colour are you today?
BRONWYN: Same as normal.
THERAPIST/CLARINETTIST: What's on your mind?

HESTER *enters and opens up the fridge to find a snack.*

BRONWYN: Oh, literally nothing! Like it's super-chill obviously…

HESTER *retreats to her bedroom.*

Like, it's about this dream.

THERAPIST/CLARINETTIST: Oh, yes? And what happened in last night's—
BRONWYN: No, not yesterday.

Beat.

It's not heavy or anything.

Beat.

There was a colourful playdough factory working away in my brain. All self-operated, like no little minions mindlessly pressing and yanking and squeezing inside my frontal lobe or anything. Just a Tetris display of unmanned shapes and surfaces and nooks and crannies chugging along in a goopy, orderly operation. The scene would unfold the same, every time. A part of the machinery, normally the drooping chandelier-shaped part, would swell and leak like a squid pissing away its ink and suddenly all hell is breaking loose and parts are jammed and clogged and compressing and boiling and *oozing*. I realise pretty quickly that the factory is not just malfunctioning, it's *destroying* itself. It's like I'm inside my own brain, watching the disaster as this omnipresent *thing*, in paralysing panic. Like there's nothing stopping what's coming.

THERAPIST/CLARINETTIST: / And how does that make you feel?
BRONWYN: Um, yeah. Not great.
THERAPIST/CLARINETTIST: Used to?

Beat.

Used to have these dreams?

BRONWYN: Yeah. Not any more.

THERAPIST/CLARINETTIST: When did they stop?

BRONWYN: When I got here. And for some odd reason, that terrifies me more.

The lights dim.

Beat.

There's a fade up and HESTER *is out of breath, staring towards the door.*

THERAPIST/CLARINETTIST: What colour are you today?

BRONWYN: Same as normal?

THERAPIST/CLARINETTIST: What's on your mind?

BRONWYN: A lot, but like, you know, that's everyone.

Lights dim, then a fade up and HESTER *is kicking off her shoes, puffed from her run.*

THERAPIST/CLARINETTIST: And how does that make you feel?

BRONWYN: It doesn't weigh on me too much.

Lights dim, then a fade up and HESTER, *shoes on, is downing some water, gasping for breath.*

THERAPIST/CLARINETTIST: And what colour are we today?

BRONWYN: It actually feels more like—

THERAPIST/CLARINETTIST: What's on your mind?

BRONWYN: Yeah, I was about to tell you—

THERAPIST/CLARINETTIST: Food for thought—

BRONWYN: I've been waiting to tell you all day—

THERAPIST/CLARINETTIST: First thought to come to mind—

BRONWYN: Mauve—

THERAPIST/CLARINETTIST: And how does that make you feel?

BRONWYN: A bit useless!

Lights dim, then a fade up and HESTER *is untying her shoes, looking down.* BRONWYN *appears in the doorway, puffed after their racewalk. The tension is musky and thick in the air.*

THERAPIST/CLARINETTIST: What's on your mind?

BRONWYN: Why am I like this?
THERAPIST/CLARINETTIST: What colour are you today?
BRONWYN: You look at me, and you see someone capable?
THERAPIST/CLARINETTIST: What colour are you today?
BRONWYN: It's like I'm one step behind and will never catch up.
THERAPIST/CLARINETTIST: And how does that make you feel?
BRONWYN: I think this is meant to be the best time of my life … ?

The lights pulse to represent a manipulation in time. A figure approaches the window and knocks, leaving behind a note. BRONWYN *approaches, opens the window and collects the note addressed to them that reads: 'I see my mother in you, every day. Like you're her, reincarnate. How lucky am I? I love you.' Audiences may or may not see this note.*

The washing machine jingles, supported by the live INSTRUMENTALISTS, *signalling a finished cycle.* HESTER *approaches the machine,* BRONWYN *still distracted by their note.*

HESTER *opens its door. She empties out the wet clothes onto the floor. Meanwhile,* BRONWYN*'s alarm goes off. Great, time to hang up their laundry.*

HESTER *returns to her work.* BRONWYN *finds their wet laundry on the floor, a failure despite their efforts. They hang up their clothes in silence.*

SCENE 7. FOOD FOR THOUGHT

The INSTRUMENTALISTS *play a rendition of 'By the Seaside', causing* HESTER *to stir, then eventually wake up. She readies herself for a run. On her way out, she bumps into a tired-eyed* BRONWYN, *who has just returned from their racewalk.*

HESTER: Whoa. Hi.
BRONWYN: Yeah, just got back.
HESTER: I don't think I've ever seen you up so early.
BRONWYN: Well, it's a big day. And I've got an appointment in a couple hours anyway.

BRONWYN *unties their shoelaces while* HESTER *attaches safety equipment.* BRONWYN *stares.*

HESTER: Knuckle lights … high-vis vest … safety alarm. Emits a hundred-and-thirty-decibel siren and flashing light.

Beat.

Sun's not up.

HESTER *begins stretching.* BRONWYN *heads to the fridge and starts gulping down water.*

BRONWYN: So you don't listen to music?

HESTER: No, no. Silence … silence is better.

BRONWYN: …

HESTER: I'm more of a podcast person actually.

BRONWYN: [*teasing, podcast voice*] 'Welcome back! And if you're along with me, congrats on making it through your intermittent fast! So … I get it. That keto grind. I'm pretty sure most of you listening are skeptics of the two a.m. workouts and carnivore dieting. I used to be too. But I'll be real with you for a second. Bone broth doesn't have to be scary. And worry not about my health, heart disease / is actually a myth'—

HESTER: I actually listen to true crime.

BRONWYN: Oh sorry— [*Resetting back into podcast voice*] 'As he hacked her body into pieces on the side of the road, he gave a limb to each of the rabid kelpies he brought in the back of his white van, it's always a / white van—'

HESTER: I literally listened to that episode the other day—

BRONWYN: I know, it kind of echoes. It was also on loop while you slept, and honestly … I don't know what's worse. Staying awake to hear about the dismemberment or fall asleep to it—

HESTER: 'Well, we will find out. Next week on the pod, with more salacious accounts of people making the most monstrous decisions and life commitments you've ever seen.'

BRONWYN: 'What does it take to con everyone you've ever known out of their money, their time, their lifeline?'

HESTER: 'What does it take to hit someone with your car and just drive away, leaving them to die?'

BRONWYN: Ooof!

HESTER: What does it take to pick out someone, not because you want to ask for their number or be their friend but because you want to whack them across the head, brain matter spraying everywhere like a faulty hose, and do whatever you want to them? What does it take to chew and tear at human meat and use the skin to make furniture? What does it take to explore the inside of a body, to dislodge, and rip, and scavenge, while it's still warm? What does it take to fill a jar to the brim with teeth and hair follicles, or let an eyeball pickle next to your cabbage, the kimchi? Serve it like a soft-boiled egg with some greens, and watch people dig in without a clue? What does it take to build the perfect place to keep someone? To be the only one in the world to know where someone is buried? To push someone off a ledge or cliff in the heat of the moment, or fantasise about it so often that you eventually just do it. Where does one even find a cliff? I want someone to stab me and I'm talking stab, like, through flesh, hard and soft flesh. Ten times over. Forty-seven. Eighty-five. Two-hundred-and-two times over, and then I want to stab them back. I'm not going to do it but I want to know how it feels. Slice and dice. Strangle. Drown. Poison. Rip. Dismember. I just want to know how it feels. Just like the tongue with all its knobbly papillae, somehow knowing what it'd be like to lick anything, literally anything. A sand-coated seashell. A mossy rock. The dusty insides of a vacuum. A rusty coin. A flaky something under a toenail. A cocktail of maggoty compost. What's it like … to go there? To say fuck intrusive … and welcome the thoughts in. Step into the unknown.

Beat.

HESTER *realises time has flown by.*

BRONWYN: Guests will be coming soon!

HESTER: Soon?! Really? How soon?

BRONWYN: Like, pretty soon.

HESTER: / I've gotta start on the croquembouche.

BRONWYN: / We've gotta start on the croquembouche.

HESTER: You remembered?

BRONWYN: Uh, yes. Is … everyone's favourite party snack, so …

HESTER: Yeah, no, I'm just. Don't know why, but I thought you were just going to chuck out some Doritos, Maltesers, popcorn, and then call it a day!

BRONWYN: Nah. I feel like a party isn't a party without a fresh-out-the-oven, doughy, / tiered, meticulously decorated, festive croquembouche.

HESTER: / tiered, meticulously decorated, festive croquembouche.

They both smile.

Great, yeah, let's make … a croquembouche.

BRONWYN: Together.

BRONWYN *appears nervous.*

HESTER: [*the whitest of lies*] It's only impressive to look at. Making it is easy.

BRONWYN *takes a breath. In comes a syncopated melodic underscore, featuring all five* INSTRUMENTALISTS. HESTER *and* BRONWYN *engage in a choreographed meal prep with polite nudges, reaching over one another, borrowing ingredients, and their overlapping bodies create a chaotic but seamless atmosphere. They reach for the bizarre bouquet, its stems blossoming into colourful eggs instead of flowers.* HESTER, *who cleans as she goes, doesn't notice* BRONWYN*'s trail of destruction that follows them. The actors may prepare an actual croquembouche.*

A silhouette of the LOVE INTEREST/ELECTRIC GUITARIST *tries to get in through the window. He wants to see* BRONWYN *but has convinced himself that the window entrance is romantic and using the door is below him. He knocks on the glass. Both* HESTER *and* BRONWYN *look to the sound.* HESTER *is on edge. Not him again. But,* BRONWYN *points to the egg bouquet.*

BRONWYN: Egg, please.

HESTER: [*pleasantly surprised*] STAT.

HESTER *eagerly grabs the egg. Together they start on the dough.*

… Um

BRONWYN: Yeah?

HESTER: [*gesturing to window*] Why does …?

BRONWYN: Oh. It's … it's romantic apparently.

The LOVE INTEREST/ELECTRIC GUITARIST *bursts into a declaration of love through song. The* NEIGHBOUR/PIANIST *suddenly appears, perky and terrifying.*

NEIGHBOUR/PIANIST: HAPPY HUMP!

Both HESTER *and* BRONWYN *jump out of their skin.*

So it's Wednesday. Are you aware it's Wednesday?

HESTER *eyes* BRONWYN, *who is oblivious.*

HESTER: Oh no.
BRONWYN: Yeah, pumped for hump!
HESTER: I'm so sorry.

The tone has shifted in the room. HESTER *is silently fuming.*

NEIGHBOUR/PIANIST: Yeah, so. In case you didn't know, we have a system here. Yes, we have a system here. And like all systems, they ensure all things run smoothly. The system of here, the system of now, the system that exists under our collective roof is that each month a certain household takes out all the bins on behalf of the entire complex. So that would mean your bins. That would mean my bins. And yes, that would mean everyone else's bins too! I'm not sure if you realise what month it is, but it's your month.
HESTER: Yes, yes our month.
NEIGHBOUR/PIANIST: I've just done it for you because there's a lot riding on this week, yes, there is. Because it's not just the all-waste, it's the recycling and the glass and also the compost. So I've sorted that one for you, alright? And I know how fickle memory can be, and how time escapes us, so I've printed out the schedule and it's by the stairs should you need it! Laminated and all, because of that pesky rain. But yes … Wednesday. It is Wednesday. Today.
HESTER: I'm sorry—
NEIGHBOUR/PIANIST: And of course next week, we are on to the next month so it won't be your responsibility for a good long while but I thought you had a right to know!

The LOVE INTEREST/ELECTRIC GUITARIST *gives up on his live composition. His shadow is seen sulking away.*

Well, I'll see you tonight!

The NEIGHBOUR/PIANIST *slinks back into their nest.*

HESTER: How did they get in here? Did you leave the door unlocked?
BRONWYN: No.
HESTER: The window?
BRONWYN: Oh, he hasn't / been over for a few days now—
HESTER: He hasn't visited? It's okay if he has and you forgot to lock up, like it's all good.
BRONWYN: He hasn't come over, like I said.
HESTER: You got the key? You didn't leave it outside for anyone to grab?

BRONWYN *brandishes the key. Confused,* HESTER *checks the front door.*

No way. It doesn't lock.

Beat.

They jam a chair up against the door, securing it in place.

… Didn't I ask you to sort the bins this week?

One egg falls onto the floor and cracks open.

BRONWYN: Yeah, I forgot. Sorrrrry.

Silence.

They both turn back to their baking.

More silence.

HESTER: … I think that's ready, for the oven I mean.
BRONWYN: Okay.
HESTER: Once I put it in the oven the whole space will be clear.
BRONWYN: Yes, it—
HESTER: Apart from your pasta. That's still there. It's June and the bowl is empty.
BRONWYN: Oh I—
HESTER: It's just seen us through an entire semester and exams …
BRONWYN: Yeah, I'm on it.
HESTER: Literally no rush, just circling back, and it's … like there's mould. And not going to lie, it baffles me that you see that every day

and don't really do anything about it … like it makes me crazy … like AHHH … like I'm a serial killer for slobs—

BRONWYN: Hahahahahaha—

HESTER *continues to work at party prep while eyeing* BRONWYN *cleaning the bowl. It is very tense and uncomfortable.* BRONWYN *feels that familiar, awful sensation washing over their body and is desperate to retreat somewhere ... for a moment.*

[*Muttering to self*] Clear the food. Clean the space. That's it. See? What's scary about that? What's hard about that? A thirty-second-long job, Bron! Do the disciplined thing …

THERAPIST/CLARINETTIST: What is on your mind?

BRONWYN: The pasta.

THERAPIST/CLARINETTIST: How does that make you feel?

BRONWYN: There's nothing to feel. I'm just cleaning the pasta.

THERAPIST/CLARINETTIST: Why didn't you clean it earlier?

HESTER *has redirected her focus from the kitchen. She is drawn to the couch like a mosquito to skin, and dives her arm into it, pulling out a popcorn kernel.*

HESTER: How was the movie?

BRONWYN: How did you know?

HESTER *continues plucking bright-purple popcorn from the couch. She plunges her arm in again, then her head, then her torso, then her legs, and suddenly she's disappeared into the couch abyss.* BRONWYN *is freaked out anew.*

You know what to do … but of course it's not working, no. My hands are sweaty but somehow like chalk and my pupils hang on to the very tips of my vision because I'll be damned if I'm gonna cry.

THERAPIST/CLARINETTIST: You've exhausted your free sessions.

BRONWYN: Riding it out is the only option, thinking about nothing or quite simply everything as my face and my voice and my limbs explain in its own pathetic way just how much I was kinda maybe not okay.

Everything is falling apart. And I'm letting it, why am I letting it?

HESTER*'s head pops up and out of the couch.*

HESTER: I'm going shopping later. Need me to get you more snacks? Popcorn?
THERAPIST/CLARINETTIST: So same time next week?
BRONWYN: No …

HESTER *re-emerges from the couch and gets up. She points to a couch cushion, which has fallen to the floor.*

HESTER: Hey, can you reset that please?
BRONWYN: Uh, you're literally right next to it … ?
HESTER: I just I can't right now, and I want to see you do it.

BRONWYN *blanches. After a moment of recovery, they position the cushion on the couch.*

Diamond.

BRONWYN *repositions the cushion on the couch, no longer a square but a diamond.*

BRONWYN: I'm going to go get ready. Someone special is coming tonight. You?

HESTER *reddens.*

SCENE 8. HOUSE-LUKEWARMING

A new score begins, featuring only the LOVE INTEREST/ELECTRIC GUITARIST, *who is roused from his nest.* BRONWYN *prepares a drink and sips nervously as they set up the space.* HESTER *brings out the croquembouche, and makes small readjustments here and there, without* BRONWYN *noticing.*

There is a knock at the door, startling them both.

HESTER: Oh…god.
BRONWYN: [*masking their nervousness*] Let's crank up the tunes.

BRONWYN *answers the door, and as they lock eyes with the* LOVE INTEREST/ELECTRIC GUITARIST. HESTER *works to avoid them. With the entrance left open, the* NEIGHBOUR/PIANIST *signals entering the space with a:*

NEIGHBOUR/PIANIST: How ergonomic!

The NEIGHBOUR/PIANIST *launches into the swing composition, coming alive from their keyboard, aka the shots table.* HESTER *approaches.*

HESTER: Welcome!

NEIGHBOUR/PIANIST: Lovely house!

HESTER: Thanks!

NEIGHBOUR/PIANIST: Lovely home!

HESTER: Thanks!

HESTER *and the* NEIGHBOUR/PIANIST *both down a shot, the swing composition becoming the slightest bit looser.*

The HANDYMAN/TROMBONIST *walks in and makes their entrance known through joining the swing composition. Both* HESTER *and* BRONWYN *lock eyes and share a moment of regret before welcoming him in.*

NEIGHBOUR/PIANIST: You fixed my showerhead!

Both the HANDYMAN/TROMBONIST *and* NEIGHBOUR/PIANIST *down a shot together and the pianist's contribution to the score becomes even looser, showing a descension in sobriety.*

The THERAPIST/CLARINETTIST *waltzes in.* HESTER *clocks this stranger and freezes, unsure of what to do.* BRONWYN *almost chokes on their drink.*

HESTER: Uh, hello! Are you lost?

THERAPIST/CLARINETTIST: Hi, good evening.

HESTER: Uh, can I help you?

THERAPIST/CLARINETTIST: What's on your mind?

HESTER: … Lots. I'm the host.

THERAPIST/CLARINETTIST: And how does that make you feel?

HESTER: …

BRONWYN *approaches.*

BRONWYN: Um, hello.

HESTER: Did we make this an open invite?

THERAPIST/CLARINETTIST: Hello, Bronwyn.

HESTER: :)

BRONWYN: [*to* HESTER] They're a … friend.

HESTER *politely yet hastily departs. The* THERAPIST/

CLARINETTIST *saunters off.*

The REAL-ESTATE AGENT/VIOLINIST *is the last to arrive, uninvited, at the very moment the music swells to a climax.*

REAL-ESTATE AGENT/VIOLINIST: Routine inspection!

They join the composition and the sound becomes full, resembling a lively, swing band in all its glory.

HESTER / BRONWYN: Now?!

The INSTRUMENTALISTS *effortlessly navigate the party space. As each musician engages with a shot, their own composition becomes less disciplined and more rowdy.*

The LOVE INTEREST/ELECTRIC GUITARIST *is glued to* BRONWYN, *who is growing more and more perturbed by his awe of them. All the while,* HESTER *engages with the* REAL-ESTATE AGENT/VIOLINIST *out of courtesy.*

HESTER: Hello! I uh, hope we've done the space justice.

REAL-ESTATE AGENT/VIOLINIST: Oh, we don't have to do this.

HESTER: What?

REAL-ESTATE AGENT/VIOLINIST: Talk about this place like it's the only thing there is to talk about. You exist outside of it don't you?

HESTER: Uh—I uh—yeah. Yes, I do.

Beat.

Would love to know more about you. What interests you?

REAL-ESTATE AGENT/VIOLINIST: Houses.

HESTER: Oh. And … ?

REAL-ESTATE AGENT/VIOLINIST: Homes.

HESTER: Oh.

As BRONWYN *speaks to the* LOVE INTEREST/ELECTRIC GUITARIST, *he gestures for them to sit on the counter. They oblige, confused. Then he ties their shoelace, barely masking how enraptured he is by his saving of them.*

BRONWYN: Oh! You're so observant. [*Icked*] Aw.

REAL-ESTATE AGENT/VIOLINIST: Don't mind me, this assessment will be done with the utmost discretion. Have your fun. [*Cheerily*] I'm a fly on the wall, you could say!

At that, the REAL-ESTATE AGENT/VIOLINIST *glides away with flare, ebbing in and out of being on the clock by parading the party dance floor.* HESTER *watches on, anxious.*

One paper suddenly flies in on a breeze and sticks to the outside of the window looking in. It's blurry, so no writing can be deciphered. No-one seems to notice.

BRONWYN *tries to walk away but the* LOVE INTEREST/ELECTRIC GUITARIST *saunters in front and rolls out a red carpet. Now,* BRONWYN *can cross, yet as they do they feel ridiculous.*

The party reaches a physical and musical climax and is immediately interrupted by the NEIGHBOUR/PIANIST *passing out, head flopping on piano keys. The musical dissonance stretches for a beat, then the power goes out in the apartment, cutting off the keyboard sound altogether.*

SCENE 9. MANY MOONS

The other INSTRUMENTALISTS *are temporarily stumped, then after a beat, they proceed with a late blues composition as they file out. As the guests do, they voice farewells like 'thanks, I'm off', 'sorry, gotta go', 'see ya', etc. This doesn't deter the* LOVE INTEREST/ELECTRIC GUITARIST, *who reaches out and grabs* BRONWYN*'s waist. He sandwiches them between him and his guitar..*

HESTER *approaches* BRONWYN.

HESTER: Bronwyn? That's you, right?
BRONWYN: You feel that?
HESTER: What?
BRONWYN: It's the end of fun.

Beat.

The LOVE INTEREST/ELECTRIC GUITARIST *plays on.*

HESTER: … So the lights! The fuse has blown or something. No lights.
BRONWYN: Weird, the weather's behaving …?
HESTER: [*patience wearing thin*] … So … / yeah I need help, thank you, Bronwyn.
BRONWYN: Do you need help?

BRONWYN *escapes and waves goodbye to the* LOVE INTEREST/ ELECTRIC GUITARIST *as he sways and plays at them.*

I actually don't know your name.

Both HESTER *and* BRONWYN *race around to gather and re-plug cables, which cause the lighting states on stage to alter. Despite their mighty effort, they fail to revive the power to the keyboard. They prod the* NEIGHBOUR/PIANIST, *who is still slumped over the keyboard.*

HESTER: [*to* LOVE INTEREST/ELECTRIC GUITARIST] Hey, take them home will you? You practically live here, so help your fellow neighbour.

LOVE INTEREST/ELECTRIC GUITARIST *starts to play a love ballad to* BRONWYN. *They snap at him, the first time ever.*

BRONWYN: It's not even in tune.

LOVE INTEREST/ELECTRIC GUITARIST *flinches. He revives the* NEIGHBOUR/PIANIST, *then sulks to his nest.*

HESTER *starts to type as* BRONWYN *stands over her. Their faces are illuminated by the screen light.*

HESTER: 'Good evening, Ma'am'—

BRONWYN: 'It has been many moons since our last communications with you'—

HESTER: 'We hope it's been filled with—

BRONWYN: 'good fortune'—

HESTER: 'and good health'—

The typing continues.

BRONWYN: 'Please.' Let's sprinkle a 'please' in maybe.

HESTER: 'Pretty please'—

BRONWYN: 'If it wouldn't be too much trouble, could you pretty please'—

HESTER: 'and you had the time on your hands, could you pretty please make arrangements to / revive our power'—

BRONWYN: 'Assess the power outage'—

HESTER: 'We'd happily remunerate you for your troubles.'

BRONWYN: 'Name the price'—

HESTER: 'Write a card of thanks'—
BRONWYN: 'We'll source one from a smaller boutique with creativity on their hands'—
HESTER: 'Take you out to dinner'—
BRONWYN: 'Shout some fruity lexia'—

HESTER *stops typing. The washing machine whirs slightly like a warning signal.*

HESTER: Uh … goon?

Beat.

BRONWYN: Oh. Uh. 'Where you'll be treated to a bottle of the very best'—
HESTER: Ooh, money, money, money … How about 'We'll treat you to the house'—
BRONWYN: 'We'll treat you to the house *wine*'—

Beat.

Please don't give them the / house—
HESTER: 'House wine'—
BRONWYN: 'And'—
HESTER: 'Invite you to our next party'—
BRONWYN: 'Don't listen to the rumours circulating about our first one'—
HESTER: Where's the house emoji? Because it's a housing matter—
BRONWYN: Where we talk about our attempts to fix it, we need one of these—

Bronwyn makes the 'curious monocle' face.

HESTER: [*making a 'winky sticking-tongue-out' face*] To show that we can be goofy too. Makes us look like fun.
BRONWYN: Actually do a house. One at the start, one at the end? Like we're bookending the message.
HESTER: Three … hearts…
BRONWYN: Bronwyn.
HESTER: Hester.

HESTER *finalises the email. She presses send. They both wait for a response from the* REAL ESTATE AGENT/VIOLINIST. *A long silence, then:*

No word back.

The REAL-ESTATE AGENT/VIOLINIST, *who has gone mostly unnoticed since the party, is heard tutting at the mess around her. She exits.*

SCENE 10. DIRTY LAUNDRY

BRONWYN *breaks the stillness by yawning, alerting* HESTER *and propelling her into a clean.*

BRONWYN: Oh, Hes. Don't you think we should leave it to the morning?
HESTER: We're both leaving for uni in the morning.
BRONWYN: Oh. Yeah. Well, after? I can do most of it when I get back.
HESTER: The stick will be harder to get out. And it'll smell of god-knows-what people brought.

Beat.

BRONWYN: [*smelling*] … ginger piss.
HESTER: You can go to bed though, it's okay.
BRONWYN: No, no, I can help.
HESTER: Sure.
BRONWYN: [*helplessly*] I can start wherever you'd like.
HESTER: Uh yeah, I reckon just pick up a cloth or bin and start cleaning. You study maps, so you should know where everything is.
BRONWYN: … Right.

Beat.

BRONWYN *starts to clean, very well-intentioned but lazy in their efforts. At some point, they start to retrieve bin bags, when* HESTER *waves them off and grabs some herself.*

HESTER: No, no, it's okay. You and bin bags don't really go together, so.

Despite her frustrations, that was meant to be a joke, but the tone has drastically shifted and BRONWYN *quickly moves on to a different chore, red in the face, more focused now on cleaning. They put a load on the washing machine. It whirs excitedly, then soon its sound takes on an unhealthy chugging that gets more and more aggressive. The live* INSTRUMENTALISTS *begin to respond by vibrating as one organism—the sound and movement intensifies gradually.* HESTER*'s side gets progressively cleaner.* BRONWYN, *who still has work to do, stops momentarily for a break.*

How are you going there, Bronwyn?

HESTER *catches* BRONWYN.

BRONWYN: …

HESTER: … It's okay / I'll do it—

BRONWYN: I'll do it, seriously, I can do it / I was just checking because my mum—

HESTER: … It's seriously no fuss I can do it, you can go to bed / and we're both happy—

BRONWYN: I'm not going to leave you to fix all this on your own—

HESTER: You already are!

The washing machine convulsions crescendo to a loud climax, then the sound ceases. It is broken.

SCENE 11. A PLEA DEAL

HESTER *and* BRONWYN *look at each other then spring into action, supported by a frantic live score by all five* INSTRUMENTALISTS.

HESTER *starts on a DIY laundry station and* BRONWYN, *thinking on their feet, yanks the* REAL-ESTATE AGENT/VIOLINIST*'s bow from her hand mid-composition.*

The violin bow becomes a makeshift laundry stick and BRONWYN *manually gets to work with the laundry that has piled up.*

HESTER *sits and opens up her laptop.* BRONWYN*'s attention is drawn to the screen light, and they nod in agreement. Yes, they need to let the* REAL ESTATE AGENT/VIOLINIST *know of this too.* HESTER *starts to type away, and* BRONWYN *joins in from across the room, still working at the laundry.*

HESTER: 'Good evening Ms … Ms,

I understand we are reaching out at an ungodly time'—

BRONWYN: Oooooh, maybe refrain from using 'un / godly'. She might be religious.

HESTER: 'Godly'—Yes, 'Godly'—

BRONWYN: 'outside of your operable hours'—

HESTER: 'outside of your operable hours'—

BRONWYN: 'although we are grateful for the partially furnished arrangement'—

HESTER: 'so incredibly blessed'—

BRONWYN: 'honoured'—

HESTER: 'what did we do to deserve furniture?'—

BRONWYN: 'the washing machine has broken down'—

BRONWYN *continues stirring the washing with the* REAL-ESTATE AGENT/VIOLINIST*'s bow.*

HESTER: 'has gone to sleep on us'—

BRONWYN: 'we're sure it's a high-calibre product'—

HESTER: 'we love it so much, it's so pretty'—

BRONWYN: 'we've had so much fun with it so far, thank you'—

HESTER: 'thank you so much'—

BRONWYN: 'without you there would be no washing machine'—

Bubbles are pouring out of the machine. BRONWYN *tries to catch them all in a hamper.*

HESTER: 'no clean clothes'—

BRONWYN: 'no hope'—

HESTER: 'we'd smell'—

BRONWYN: 'so thank you'—

HESTER: 'we owe you one' / reword—

BRONWYN: reword—

HESTER: 'we owe you more than we could ever give'—

BRONWYN: 'we owe you our lives'—

HESTER: 'so incredibly sorry to pester you after all you've done for us'—

BRONWYN: 'all you continue to do for us' / better—

HESTER: better—

BRONWYN *slips and falls in the bubble mess.*

'we don't deserve you'—

BRONWYN: 'would you be ever so kind as to'—
HESTER: 'THE BIGGEST SOLID'—
BRONWYN: 'make arrangements to fix this'—

BRONWYN *lays pathetically on the floor in the mess.*

HESTER: 'love you'—
BRONWYN: 'we insist that you forward us the invoice'—
HESTER: 'this is our mess, not yours'—
BRONWYN: 'at your earliest convenience'—
HESTER: 'LOVE YOU'—
BRONWYN: 'come after five, we'll be home'—
HESTER: 'I love you so fucking much'—
BRONWYN: 'come at midnight, we'll be up'—
HESTER: 'what would we do without you'—
BRONWYN: 'unannounced at three a.m. … hell, we can be up for that too'—
HESTER: 'don't be a stranger'—
BRONWYN: Bron.
HESTER: Hes.
BRONWYN: / x x x—
HESTER: / x x x x—
BRONWYN: [*stopping* HESTER] No no. Too much.

HESTER *nods aggressively, agreeing. She removes an 'x'. And sends. They both wait.*

Nothing.

There's a lonesome quiet that settles over the room. HESTER *shuts her laptop, and* BRONWYN *ceases to do the laundry. They are both exhausted. The remaining* INSTRUMENTALISTS *begin a live composition that sounds like it is also on its last leg.*

A moment of peace, then:

Suddenly, a section of the roof caves in, trapping the HANDYMAN/TROMBONIST, *severing his live sound. An overwhelming amount of eviction notices fall from the ceiling that no-one has noticed yet.*

SCENE 12. CONFESSIONARY

HESTER*, no longer surprised at the presence of another house malfunction, reopens her laptop, beginning what she knows is her last email to the* REAL ESTATE AGENT/VIOLINIST. BRONWYN *retreats to their bed, desperate to hide from the mounting disaster.*

HESTER: 'Ms.

I won't lie to you. There's a hole in the ceiling. Gaping. It fell onto someone, they might be dead. They might not be. But more than that, we would be ever-so-grateful for a repair within the week. Speaking of repairs, I believe the person that was flattened is your go-to guy. So, don't waste your time calling them, I reckon.

I know this doesn't reflect well on us. Three consecutive emails admitting to damages. I should be better at this. *Living* here. But it seems all I do is mess everything up, even though I've had like two decades of experience. I tried though … unpacking the most *me* things first, the knick-knacks. Framed pictures, books, games … fridge magnets. I thought, 'There I am! And *there,* and *there*. *Truly* settled'. But … well … I never stopped feeling like an intruder. Like, I'm indebted to someone, like that *someone* is right on the other side of the door ready to take back what's theirs. I anticipate that knock all the time. Telling me it's *time to go*. Well, when it is, fingers crossed it's quick … make it quick. Oh and I obsess over how so out-of-pocket I am and whether that's a fair trade for creaky floors, faulty sinks, no-lock doors, and a double bed posing as two single trundles. And, sometimes, I'm just so *angry*, the kind of angry like you've had a long day and nothing's gone right and you finally stub your toe and you're just '*fucking FUCKING ugghh*' at an empty room and swinging your limbs around like you can bat away the *unfairness* of it all. Paycheck to paycheck and a dying house, that's my lot in life right now.

[*Recovering all professionalism*] My hope here is that you'd respect my candour. I know building relationships based on a foundation of lies doesn't bode well for either party.

Hope to hear back from you at some point in the near future.

Thank you. In advance. Unless you do nothing. Then I retract.

HESTER *sends the email. Waits. No response. She is no longer surprised.*

SCENE 13. ROOMMATE SHOWDOWN

In the moonlight, HESTER *begins trying to clean the space.* BRONWYN *wakes and stands, anxiety setting in. The lights are out, a section of the ceiling destroyed, and more mess to clean.* HESTER *accidentally destroys the croquembouche.* BRONWYN *whizzes around, and in an unexpected twist,* HESTER *is not the one to snap.*

BRONWYN: GREAT! Thanks, hello to you too, Hester. What a perfect place for our fresh-out-the-oven, doughy, tiered, meticulously decorated, festive croque-of-SHIT! But you know what?! I'll give you some credit. At least it's you making a mess of it all this time. Phew, Hester isn't a robot! This isn't working, this isn't working, THIS— [*gesturing between herself and* HESTER] isn't working. The way you walk around all smug, acting like without your attentive, heroic, blessed touch the very bones of this place will collapse in on us and cease to function. Well, you know what? You're here and things are falling to shit. Even on the days I think I'm getting it all right I'm getting it wrong. It's abundantly clear what you think of me, especially when you're racing out the house for a leisurely run as I'm leaving for my hardcore racewalk, making a point to overtake me, which isn't hard to do by the way. Like, I'm limited by needing one foot on the ground at all times and you have the freedom to do a bloody cartwheel if you feel so inclined. I haven't conveniently forgotten that you used to run in the mornings but like a goddamn menstrual cycle you just had to sync up with my schedule. Dressed in your stupid high-vis, with your stupid weapons waiting … actually, hoping for something to come and HURT YOU.

As BRONWYN *unleashes on* HESTER*, eviction notices, blurry and indistinguishable, thud and stick to the outside of the window.*

Beat.

This is my home.

HESTER *stands, red in the face, tears in the eyes.*

HESTER: This is my home too.
BRONWYN: I know that, but a home should be lived in.
HESTER: A home should be livable.

BRONWYN: You can live in a little bit of mess.
HESTER: You can wash a couple of dishes.
BRONWYN: It's more than just the dishes.
HESTER: I know—that's the problem.

They both feel like they should say sorry, but neither do.

Silence.

They are interrupted by the doorbell once more. Eviction notices slide under the door, and appear from other parts of the apartment. The pair are left in shock, unable to clear the air. The damage is done and there is no foreseeable resolution.

SCENE 14. MOVE OUT

HESTER *and* BRONWYN *reluctantly pack up their belongings,* BRONWYN *collecting everything purple and* HESTER *gathering everything orange.*

Meanwhile, the REAL-ESTATE AGENT/VIOLINIST*'s voice echoes.*

REAL-ESTATE AGENT/VIOLINIST: To whom this may concern, thank you for your correspondence. I was attending a very important function when this communication attempt was made. Additionally, I'm sure you understand that contacting me outside of my office hours is not very feasible. It's, quite frankly, annoying. As specified on page seventy-eight of your contract, I have a multi-day processing time between receiving correspondence and responding to said correspondence. Nonetheless, our team has received your concerns and have made arrangements to resolve the matter aptly and without fuss.

Leave. Now, please. And in future, check your junk mail.

HESTER *and* BRONWYN *silently exit through opposite doors, a stark light washing over the space, draining it of life and colour.*

Oh, hello there. We care, we *care so deeply about you, oh, so, so, so deeply*. We understand that searching for the right rental property to call home was time-consuming and stressful but that's all over now. You have really hit the jackpot.

The REAL-ESTATE AGENT/VIOLINIST *enters, all beauty and*

charm.

This place … has a roof. This place has walls. And yes, a state-of-the-art skylight, what a feature.

The only thing left undisturbed is an almost-empty wine bottle from the housewarming, lonely on a table. The REAL-ESTATE AGENT/VIOLINIST *ties a ribbon around the stem, and places a card next to it; ready for the next tenant.*

Blackout.

THE END

The Roof is Caving In

written by **Matilda Gibbs**
with **Belle Hansen** and **Jack Burmeister**

May 8 - May 19, 2024 at La Mama Courthouse

Hester: Marlena Thomson
Bronwyn: Bek Schilling
Real Estate Agent/Violinist: Joanna Halliday
Love Interest/Electric Guitartist: Linus Finn Mackie
Neighbour/Pianist: Karen Yee
Handyman/Trombonist: Joshua Mackie
Therapist/Clarinettist: Daniel Kim

Director, Belle Hansen
Composer and Sound Designer, Jack Burmeister
Lighting Designer, Aron Murray
Stage Manager and Co-Set Designer, Brigette Jennings
Assistant Stage Manager, Jade Hibbert

CREATOR'S ACKNOWLEDGEMENT

This work was developed with the support of City of Melbourne. Special thanks go to:

Phoebe Grant, Eleanor Golding, Erin Perrey, Myf Hocking, Ryan Henry, Morgan Rose, Flick and many more who read drafts and gave feedback across the work's development.

The Team at La Mama, especially Caitlin Dullard for programming *The Roof is Caving In* at La Mama Courthouse, as part of the La Mama Learning Program, and Maureen Hartley for continuous application, editorial and educational support. Also thanks to La Mama's Designer Adam Cass.

And finally, Claire Grady, Elizabeth Arrigo and the Team at Currency Press for all their assistance with the publication of this book.

WRITER'S NOTES

The Roof Is Caving In was born out of the belief that you are never ready for adulthood, that housemate dynamics and rental environments are specific and universal types of experiences. It's treading water. It's trial and error. Sometimes their mistakes, sometimes yours. After a time, as endurance and experience builds, you're better equipped and it's easier. But there are unavoidable bumps. There's compromise and trying to meet standards, trying to communicate standards. Passive aggression, aloofness, excruciating politeness, outbursts, anxiety, nitpicking, tiptoeing. And oftentimes, the place you've signed to lease isn't making it any easier for you. I thought, "what a fun thing to write about!". And layering it with surrealism lends itself to how disoriented and exasperated we are left to feel in these sorts of living situations. These realities, although uncomfortable, are a learning curve and not necessarily a bad thing. I also see the importance in exploring the whiplash of the current rental market, how it's not operating in the interests of the next generation of homeowners. An out-of-the-blue eviction, despite the heavy surrealism, is a common experience.

Frenzy Theatre Co's ethos is centred around explosive physical theatre, and so my aim was always to honour that with a complementary frenetic, organised chaos in the dialogue. Everything from the set, to the character relationships, to the composition, to the rules of the world, have an impractical functionality that links them. Frenzy is also drawn to exploring the uncomfortable reality of life itself—for this particular work, it's the precariousness of 'home' as a young adult.

It was important to me that the characters seesaw back and forth between being pitied or understood, to being resented or condemned by the audience. Hester isn't the villain. Bronwyn isn't the villain. And with that in mind, this theatre style is Australian Gothic. The house is intrinsically a character and the true antagonist of the world. It's homely-made-unhomely, and as a landscape, its behaviour and decisions are demonstrated through the extra characters (instrumentalists). Their existence as both musicians and characters simultaneously lends itself to the surrealism of the show, as they ebb and flow out of Hester and Bronwyn's ether.

My approach to writing *The Roof is Caving In* was largely research-based. More specifically, I pigeon-holed Thomas Kilmann's conflict management types, for character-building. It identifies five possible conflict management types in someone: Accommodating, Avoiding, Compromising, Collaborating, and Competing. I feel like no one character in the play demonstrates solely one management type. This meant I could use this as an impetus in my writing to build tension and momentum.

When they first meet, I knew the housemates would be extremely accommodating to one another, to the point of them appeasing each other with a house luke-warming that, secretly, neither of them wanted. For Hester, there's a layer of Competing that presents itself more potently as time goes on. For Bronwyn, we see someone appear more Avoidant with rising conflict and as they become more vocal, Compromising—trying to be diplomatic but not a pushover.

I thought about the apartment they were living in—Belle Hansen (Director) and I knew we wanted that Australian

Gothic style embedded into the play. The limits of surrealism are truly endless, so I asked myself, "what can the apartment do to appear as hostile and ill-intentioned as possible?" An impractical layout for one. Faulty appliances. Overbearing neighbours. A front door that doesn't lock! Giant dead rats. Power outages. A questionable couch that may or may not be a disgusting portal into some awful unknown. And then, there were the ones that didn't make the cut. The house flooding. Obnoxious mould spreading. Continuous rent increases.

The process of writing this work wasn't a solo mission. Working closely with the director (Belle Hansen) and the dramaturg (Phoebe Grant) has been a godsend in bettering this script. It makes me less indulgent in content creation, and inviting others to critique and challenge my writing is my biggest takeaway for future projects. We hope you enjoy the mess we've made.

Matilda Gibbs
Playwright

COMPOSER'S NOTES

The compositions written for *The Roof is Caving In* needed to be unapologetically present and compound the tension and friction of the relationship between Hester and Bronwyn.

The music frequently blurs the line between being diegetic and non-diegetic. Non-diegetic sound does not exist within the world of the play, whereas diegetic sound is heard and acknowledged by the characters. The music works to underscore certain scenes, helping to establish the mood and accentuate the action of the scene. Then there are moments where the music shifts to becoming diegetic within the world of the play, for instance, the Love Interest communicates exclusively with Bronwyn through his guitar playing.

Compositionally, the music frequently employs polyphony, intertwining multiple independent lines that weave, intersect, and harmonise to create dense sound textures. Individual melodies emerge and recede into the background, like a pulse, coming to the forefront of your attention before rejoining the overall sound texture. This is then juxtaposed with moments of unity, where all the instruments are playing together. This enforces melodic themes that are being explored in each composition, creating a strong foundation and a sense of cohesion within the music.

Jack Burmeister
Composer

DIRECTOR'S NOTES

The Roof is Caving In is a play that can function in any surreal maximalist world … that contains the listed furniture. For our version it is bright, anxiety filled and incredibly fast-paced.
In true Australian Gothic style, Hester and Bronwyn are at the mercy of the landscape around them. This is driven by the instrumentalists who are built into the set and bring the space to life with their music, action and often ominous presence. This work comes with many exciting challenges for the performers and creative team, including long passages of interwoven simultaneous monologue, movement sequences timed to a complex live score, and visually demonstrating the large passage of time that the work is set across.
In the rehearsal room, we begin working through the text non-linearly, focusing on blocking the small interwoven arcs in the same session. A clear demonstration of this being the repeated emails, making sure that they, as a stand-alone, build in intensity and become increasingly dynamic until there is no turning point. Inside of this, I like to think of every few lines as its own little vignette, making sure that there are no passages of text that feel washed over or momentumless. Audiences are smart and our challenge with this work is to make sure the audience is always surprised by an element of what happens next, which is unbelievably enjoyable to tackle.

Belle Hansen
Director

CEO & Director – Caitlin Dullard
Marketing and Communications Manager – Georgina Capper
Development & Pathways Manager – Myf Powell
Venue Technical Manager – Hayley Fox
Acting Venue Technical Manager – Shane Grant
Producer – Amber Hart
First Nations Producer / Curator – Glenn Shea
Learning Producer & School Publications Coordinator - Maureen Hartley
Ticketing & FOH Supervisors – AYA & Gemma Horbury
Design & Marketing Admin – Adam Cass
Online Producer – Ruiqi Fu
Curators:
Gemma Horbury (Musica); Amanda Anastasi (Poetica)
Isabel Knight (Cabaretica); Sophia Constantine (La Mama for Kids), Emma Fawcett (La Mama Scratch)
Documentation – Darren Gill

COMMITTEE OF MANAGEMENT: Richard Watts (Chair), Helen Hopkins (Dep Chair), Ben Grant, (Treasurer) Caitlin Dullard (Secretary), Members - Caroline Lee, David Geoffrey Hall, Kim Ho, Beng Oh and Mark Williams.

La Mama Theatre is on traditional Land of the people of the Kulin Nation. We give our respect to the Elders of these traditional Lands, and to all First Nations people, past and present, and future. We acknowledge all events take place on stolen Lands and that sovereignty was never ceded.

La Mama is financially assisted by Creative Victoria (Creative Enterprises Program), and the City of Melbourne (Arts and Creative Partnership Program). We are grateful to all our philanthropic partners and donors, advocates, volunteers, audiences, artists and our entire community. Thank you!

La Mama Theatre & Office is at 205 Faraday St,
Carlton VIC 3053
La Mama Courthouse Theatre, 349 Drummond Street,
Carlton VIC 3053

Tel (03) 9347 6948; Office hours Mon–Fri, 11am–4pm.

www.lamama.com.au
Facebook: lamama.theatre
instagram: lamamatheatre
email: info@lamama.com.au
twitter: LaMamaTheatre

Frenzy Theatre Co

Frenzy Theatre Co is an independent organisation with a focus on creating opportunities for early career artists to create professional standard work. The company has worked with hundreds of early career artists since it was established in 2020 through developments and residency programs and new works. Frenzyís work is pop culture-based, and grounded in its commitment to dynamic physical theatre, ensemble devising and maximalism.

FRENZY
Theatre Co.

Matilda Gibbs

Playwright

MATILDA GIBBS (she/her) is a British-Australian actor and performer, originally from Chesham, England and now based in Naarm. She graduated from the Victorian College of the Arts with a Bachelor of Fine Arts (Theatre) in 2020. A co-founder and company artist of Frenzy Theatre Co, Matilda values a multi-disciplinary practice in her acting, devising, movement and writing work. She's attracted to boldness and ugliness. Her recent theatre credits are *The Exact Dimensions of Hell* (dir. Alice Darling) at fortyfivedownstairs and *SLUTNIK™: Planet of the Incels* (dir.Tansy Gorman) at TheatreWorks.

Belle Hansen

Director / Writer

BELLE HANSEN is a director and theatre maker originally from Queensland and now based in Melbourne. She has devised and directed new work with companies across Australia including Queensland Theatre, Zen Zen Zo Physical Theatre, Theatre Works and Rawcus. She is a graduate of VCA with a Bachelor of Fine Arts (Theatre) and the co-founder and artistic director of Frenzy Theatre Co. She is passionate about creating space for early career artists to explore their discipline and championing the new voices of the future.

Jack Burmeister
Composer & Sound Designer

JACK BURMEISTER is a Composer and Sound Designer who is passionate about finding synergy between his work and other forms of media. Using elements of orchestral, acoustic, electronic, and choral textures, Jack creates diverse sonic soundscapes to enhance the atmosphere and mood in any given work.

Aron Murray
Lighting Designer

ARON MURRAY is an emerging designer with a passion for the visual and a drive to create immersive designs for live performance. Receiving his formal performing arts training from the National Institute of Dramatic Art (NIDA), Aron holds a Master of Fine Art in Design for Performance as well as a Bachelor of Fine Art in Technical Theatre and Stage Management.

Brigette Jennings

Stage Manager & Co-Set Designer

BRIGETTE JENNINGS is an early-career stage manager and theatre-maker based in Naarm (Melbourne). She has been performing, working on stage and backstage since 2014 in school and community theatre. Most recently, Brigette has worked on *Bluey's Big Play* touring to QPAC in Brisbane.

Marlena Thomson

Hester

MARLENA THOMSON is a Naarm based actor, singer and dancer originally from the Blue Mountains. A graduate from the Victorian College of the Arts, Marlena has performed in a wide range of musicals, original works and plays since she was young and is thrilled to be playing the role of Hester.

Bek Schilling

Bronwyn

BEK SCHILLING is a multidisciplinary queer artist based in Naarm. Bek is a graduate of Federation University Arts Academy, trained with the Australian Shakespeare Company in their Graduate Players program, and regularly performs with Homegrown. Highlights include *Bearded* (Frankston Arts Centre), *Voyagers* (La Mama), and *You're A Catch, Why Are You Single?* (TheatreWorks).

Joanna Halliday

Real Estate Agent / Violinist

JOANNA HALLIDAY was born and raised in Naarm / Melbourne, and has studied both Music Theatre and Acting, graduating from The VCA in 2018. Joanna made her theatre debut as Juliet in Melbourne Shakespeare Company's *Romeo and Juliet* and her Feature Film debut as Young Bernadette in *Ride Like a Girl*. She has toured around Australia and the USA as Bluey and Bingo in *Bluey's Big Play*. She also appeared as Carmel in *Miss Fisher's Modern Murder Mysteries*. Joanna's passion is in physical theatre and she is very excited to be working with Frenzy Theatre Company.

Karen Yee

Neigbour / Pianist

KAREN YEE is an actor-musician who graduated from the Howard Fine Acting Studio full-time course in 2023. She is a multi-instrumentalist (piano, violin, singing, conducting) in diverse musical styles including classical, jazz, folk, rock and musical theatre. Karen is delighted to be making her Melbourne stage debut with Frenzy Theatre Company.

Linus Finn Mackie

Love Interest / Electric Guitarist

LINUS FINN MACKIE is a Melbourne-based guitarist with his roots in the live music scene. Since 2020, he has joined the ranks of several local bands like Holly Hebe, Mae Mobly and The Staples. He has also done pit work for Melbourne-based productions of *Spamalot*, *Jesus Christ Superstar* and *Mamma Mia*.

Joshua Mackie

Handyman / Trombonist

JOSHUA MACKIE is a Naarm / Melbourne based musician, actor and professional miscreant. He spends much of his time studying Jazz and Improvisation on the trombone at Melbourne University but simultaneously loves to involve himself in any and all things performative and creative. The stranger, the better.

Daniel Kim

Therapist / Clarinettist

DANIEL KIM is a Naarm / Melbourne-based performer, director, and award-winning vocal arranger. Eclectically trained, Daniel's performer credits include: a chorister in *The Hunchback of Notre Dame* (OSMaD); and *Steven in In Transit* (Lightbox Productions). His directing credits include: co-director/ MD of *Blue to the Horizon* (Sevenfold Theatre); and AMD of *Legally Blonde* (Waterdale).

Standing Ovation for
Australia's Home of Independent Theatre

In 2024, La Mama celebrates 57 years of nurturing new Australian Theatre, fearlessly facilitating independent theatre making.

Built in 1883 for Anthony Reuben Ford, a Carlton printer, the original building in Faraday Street had been used as a workshop, a boot and shoe factory, an electrical engineering workshop and a silk underwear factory before becoming a theatre in 1967. It was established by Betty Burstall and modelled on experimental theatre activities in New York. Jack Hibberd's play *Three Old Friends* was the first play performed in the tiny space. Since that time the crowded intimacy of La Mama has provided welcome opportunities to a host of playwrights, actors, directors, technicians, film-makers, poets and comedians, such as David Williamson, Barry Dickins, John Romeril, Tes Lyssiotis, Lloyd Jones, the Cantrills, Judith Lucy, Richard Frankland, Julia Zemiro, and Cate Blanchett… the list of both new and experienced theatre makers, and those artists who have been nurtured there, is long.

I set La Mama up, as a space for writers and directors to perform in but also it was a space where people came, as audience, to participate in the creative experiment...

—Betty Burstall, 1987

La Mama Theatre—which on various occasions has been called headquarters, the shopfront and the birthplace of Australian Theatre—was classified by the National Trust in 1999.

The two-storey brick building is of State cultural significance because it has been occupied by La Mama Theatre...The building is indelibly associated with the performance arts and is a rare manifestation of an experimental theatre in Australia...

—National Trust Classification Report

Sadly our home in Faraday Street burned down in May 2018 and, while we were in the process of rebuilding, our home was La Mama Courthouse on Drummond Street Carlton.

Happily, like a phoenix rising from the ashes, our rebuilt La Mama Theatre was reopened in December, 2021 with the War-Rak / Banksia Festival. (For rebuild details see https://lamama.com.au/rebuild-la-mama)

During its 50-plus years, La Mama has presented approximately 2,500 shows, and we now average around 50 primary production seasons annually, as well as developments, seasonal La Mamica events (Musica, Poetica, Cabaretica, Kids' shows), regular touring through our Mobile program, plus our VCE Learning productions, play readings, and many other special events.

Performances take place again in the restored La Mama, and continue at our second performance venue, the refurbished La Mama Courthouse, 349 Drummond Street.

An ever-increasing audience is drawn to La Mama productions, not only from the Carlton and Melbourne University environs, but from far and wide across the country.

La Mama continues to be an open, accessible space, actively breaking down barriers to the Arts through diverse programs, creative initiatives, affordable ticketing, improved accessible amenities and a welcoming ethos, for performers and audience alike, that has developed over the past five decades. La Mama is home to many and open to all.

For details of all productions and events, and bookings visit: www.lamama.com.au

Welcome to the Apartment

J Burmeister

Cl. in B♭
Tbn.
E. Gtr
Pno
Vln
mp
f
ff
Ped.
C
Light, sneaky, cheeky
Light, sneaky, cheeky

15
Cl. in B♭
Tbn.
E. Gtr
Pno
Vln
f
mp
18
D
mf
ff
Gm
Dm7/F

22
Cl. in B♭
Tbn.
E. Gtr
Gm
Dm7/F
Gm
Dm7/F
Pno
Vln
mf
f
ff
26
Gm add9

Apartment Inspection

J Burmeister

A ♩ = 90

Clarinet in B♭
mf *f* *mp* *mp*

Trombone
mf *f* *mp*

Electric Guitar
mf *f* *mp*

Piano
mf *f* *mp*
mf *f* *mp*
Ped.

Violin
mf *f* *mp*

9
B
Cl. in B♭
Tbn.
E. Gtr
Pno
Vln
fp
mf
fp
mf
mf
mf
mf
mf
mf

13
C
Cl. in B♭
Tbn.
E. Gtr
Pno
Vln
p
mp
p
mp
p
mp
p
mp
p
mp
p
mp

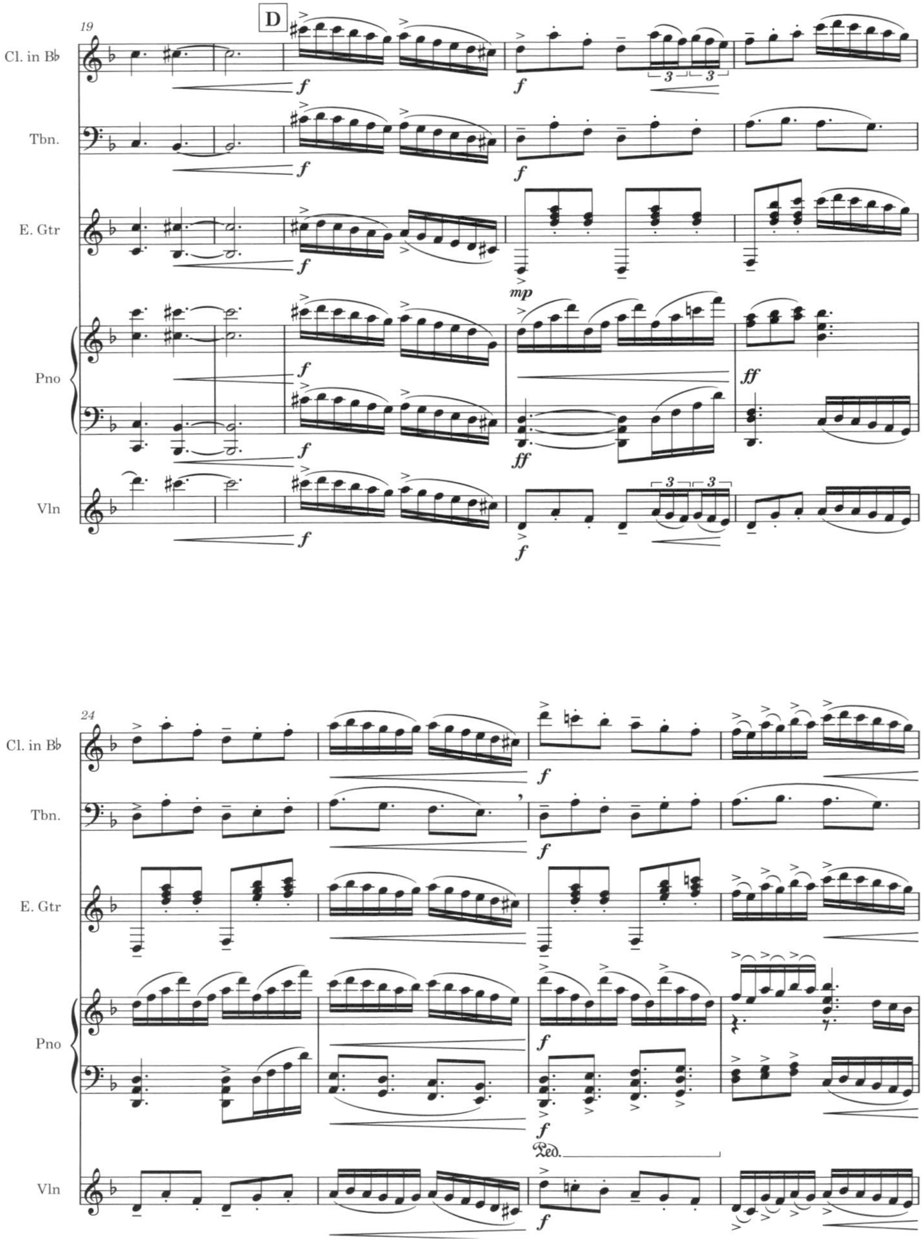

19

D

Cl. in B♭

Tbn.

E. Gtr

Pno

Vln

28
E
Cl. in B♭
Tbn.
E. Gtr
Pno
Vln
mp
fp
fp

32
Cl. in B♭
Tbn.
E. Gtr
Pno
Vln
mf
f
ff